Flight to FREEDOM!

NICKOLAS FLUX and the Underground Railroad

BY Mari Bolte
ILLUSTRATED BY Mark Simmons

CONSULTANT:
Richard Bell, PhD
Associate Professor of History
University of Maryland, College Park

GRAPHIC LIBRARY

CAPSTONE PRESS
a capstone imprint

Graphic Library is published by Capstone Press,
1710 Roe Crest Drive, North Mankato, Minnesota 56003
www.capstonepub.com

Library of Congress Cataloging-in-Publication Data
Bolte, Mari.
  Flight to freedom! : Nickolas Flux and the Underground Railroad / by
Mari Bolte ; illustrated by Mark Simmons.
    pages cm.—(Graphic library. Nickolas Flux history chronicles)
  Includes bibliographical references and index.
  Summary: "In graphic novel format, follows the adventures of Nickolas
Flux as he travels back in time and must survive a journey on the
Underground Railroad"—Provided by publisher.
  ISBN 978-1-4914-0254-2 (library binding)
  ISBN 978-1-4914-0259-7 (paperback)
  ISBN 978-1-4914-0263-4 (eBook PDF)
1. Underground Railroad—Juvenile literature. 2. Underground
Railroad—Comic books, strips, etc. 3. Fugitive slaves—United
States—History—19th century—Juvenile literature. 4. Fugitive
slaves—United States—History—19th century—Comic books, strips,
etc. 5. Antislavery movements—United States—History—19th
century—Juvenile literature. 6. Antislavery movements—United
States—History—19th century—Comic books, strips, etc. 7. Graphic
novels. I. Simmons, Mark, illustrator. II. Title.
  E450.B68 2015
  973.7'115—dc 3   2014003772

Photo Credits:
Design Elements: Shutterstock (backgrounds)

EDITOR
Christopher L. Harbo

ART DIRECTOR
Nathan Gassman

DESIGNER
Ashlee Suker

PRODUCTION SPECIALIST
Jennifer Walker

COVER ARTIST
Dante Ginevra

Printed in the United States of America in Stevens Point, Wisconsin.
032014   008092WZF14

TABLE OF CONTENTS

INTRODUCING ...

NICKOLAS FLUX

WILLIAM

CHAPTER ONE

HANDS-ON HISTORY

Sparta Hills Museum of History

Explore the exhibits, everyone! Look with your eyes, and feel with your hands! This is a hands-on history experience!

Check out these old clothes, Nick!

How do I look, Nadia?

Can you imagine living back in the 1850s?

No way. This dress is so tight!

CHAPTER TWO

RUN FOR YOUR LIFE!

Kentucky, just south of the Ohio River, 1856

Whoa! Where am I?

WOOF
WOOF

Are you ... running from something?

Please don't let them get me!

Who? What are you talking about?

Oof!

There's no time to explain. I have to run, or they'll catch me.

All right, let's go!

8

FLUX FACT

Historians estimate that around 100,000 people escaped slavery between the years 1790 and 1860. Approximately 40,000 escaped across the Ohio River.

FLUX FACT

The Fugitive Slave Act of 1850 made it easier for slave owners to recapture runaway slaves. It required citizens in all states to detain runaway slaves. The act forced many runaway slaves to flee all the way to Canada to find true freedom.

I hear someone—stay down!

Don't be afraid. My name is Greta. Come with me.

Where are you taking us?

To the conductor.

A slave and a conductor? I guess that makes me a passenger on the Underground Railroad!

Oh, no!

What's wrong?

I hear riders approaching. Stay down and keep quiet.

No sign of him, Naylor.

Keep looking! William is valuable. He must have run off with someone. That's theft, and we shoot thieves around here.

12

FLUX FACT

Kentucky was the last slave state runaways passed through before entering the North. About 300 slaves escaped through Kentucky to Ohio every year during the height of the Underground Railroad.

FLUX FACT

Some people actually traveled from the North into the South to look for slaves seeking freedom. These brave individuals were called "pilots" on the Underground Railroad.

FLUX FACT

The Underground Railroad ran both ways. Bounty hunters and kidnappers captured free blacks and runaway slaves in the North. They took them to the South and sold them back into slavery.

FLUX FACT

Conductors on the Underground Railroad faced great personal risk. They could lose their money, their homes, and even their lives. For their own safety, few records were kept. Some conductors used fake names and secret identities.

FLUX FACT

People found to be aiding escaped slaves were punished. They could be arrested, thrown in jail, or branded. A brand of "S.S." stood for "slave stealer."

FLUX FACT

Former slave Harriet "Moses" Tubman made 19 trips into the South in 10 years. She brought more than 300 slaves to freedom. Her nickname, "Moses," came from the Bible prophet who led his people to freedom.

THE FIRST SLAVES

The first slaves arrived in Virginia in 1619. By 1790 nearly 20 percent of the 3.9 million people living in the United States were slaves.

THE COTTON GIN

The African slave trade began to decline by the Revolutionary War (1775–1783). However, the invention of the cotton gin in 1793 changed things. This machine quickly separated cotton fibers from cotton seeds. Cotton became the main crop grown in the South. Plantation owners needed slaves to work the cotton fields.

SMUGGLING SLAVES

The African slave trade was banned in 1808. However, slaves were still smuggled into the country. And those already in the country—and the children they had—were still kept as slaves.

RAILROAD ORIGINS

The Underground Railroad first began in the mid-1810s. It became more organized in the late 1830s when a man named Robert Purvis formed an organization to help runaway slaves. People who helped slaves escape started to think of the safe houses as stations, or stops, on a railroad line.

NAMING THE RAILROAD

Legend says that the Underground Railroad got its name in 1831. That year a slave named Tice Davids crossed the Ohio River. His owner was not far behind. When Davids reached the Ohio shore, he disappeared. His master told people that Davids must have escaped on an "underground railroad."

FAMOUS CONDUCTORS

Conductors on the Underground Railroad helped thousands of slaves escape to freedom. Robert Purvis and Levi Still helped at least 9,000 slaves each. Levi Coffin and Thomas Garrett aided another 6,000 total. John Rankin and his family helped around 2,000 escapees.

TENSION OVER SLAVERY

Disagreements over slavery created tension between northern and southern states. In 1860 South Carolina became the first southern state to secede from the Union. Ten other states would later secede as well. These states formed the Confederate States of America. The war between the Union and the Confederate States became known as the Civil War (1861–1865).

FREEDOM

In 1862 the Union announced that any black men who enlisted during the Civil War would be given certificates of freedom. The next year President Abraham Lincoln released the Emancipation Proclamation. This document granted freedom to all slaves in Confederate territory. The 13th Amendment abolished slavery in the United States in 1865.

GLOSSARY

ABOLISH (uh-BOL-ish)—to put an end to something

AUCTION (AWK-shuhn)—a sale during which items are sold to the person who offers the most money

BRAND (BRAND)—to mark the skin with a hot iron, sometimes as a mark of disgrace

CONDUCTOR (kuhn-DUK-tuhr)—a person who helped runaway slaves escape to the North on the Underground Railroad

DETAIN (di-TAYN)—to hold someone back when he or she wants to go

EMANCIPATION (i-MAN-si-pay-shuhn)—freedom from slavery or control

FUGITIVE (FYOO-juh-tiv)—someone who is running from the law

PILOT (PYE-luht)—a person who traveled into slave states to find slaves who were seeking freedom

PLANTATION (plan-TAY-shuhn)—a large farm where crops such as cotton and sugarcane are grown; before 1865 plantations were run by slave labor

PROPERTY (PROP-ur-tee)—a physical object that belongs to someone

PROPHET (PROF-it)—a person who claims to be a messenger of God

SECEDE (si-SEED)—to formally withdraw from a group or an organization, often to form another organization

READ MORE

BAUMANN, SUSAN K. *Harriet Tubman: Conductor of the Underground Railroad.* Jr. Graphic African-American History. New York: PowerKids Press, 2014.

MCDONOUGH, YONA ZELDIS. *What Was The Underground Railroad?* What Was …? New York: Grosset & Dunlap, 2013.

WHELAN, GLORIA, AND GWENYTH SWAIN. *Voices for Freedom.* American Adventures. Ann Arbor, Mich.: Sleeping Bear Press, 2013.

INTERNET SITES

FactHound offers a safe, fun way to find Internet sites related to this book. All sites on FactHound have been researched by our staff.

Here's all you do:

Visit *www.facthound.com*

Type in this code: 9781491402542

Super-cool stuff! Check out projects, games and lots more at **www.capstonekids.com**

INDEX

ABOUT THE AUTHOR

Mari Bolte is an author of children's books and a lover of history. A degree in anthropology has given her an appreciation for other people in other times. She lives in southern Minnesota with her husband and daughter.